NEW EDITION

The Complete Keyboard Player Songbook 1

T0056624

Published by
Hal Leonard

Exclusive Distributors:
Hal Leonard
7777 West Bluemound Road,
Milwaukee, WI 53213
Email: info@halleonard.com

Hal Leonard Europe Limited
42 Wigmore Street,
Marylebone, London WIU 2 RY
Email: info@halleonardeurope.com

Hal Leonard Australia Pty. Ltd.
4 Lentara Court, Cheltenham,
Victoria 9132, Australia
Email: info@halleonard.com.au

Order No. AM1008216
ISBN 978-1-78305-428-2

Edited by Jenni Norey.
Music processed by Paul Ewers Music Design.

Printed in the EU.

www.halleonard.com

5 Years Time

Words & Music by Charlie Fink

Voice: **Flute**
Rhythm: **Funk Rock**
Tempo: ♩ = 108

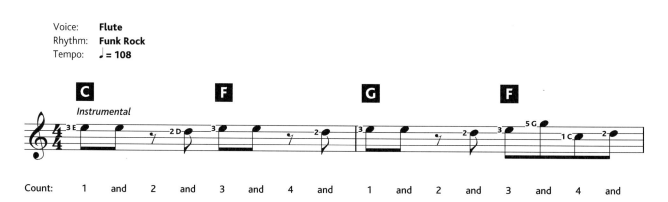

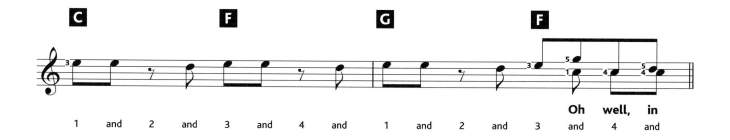

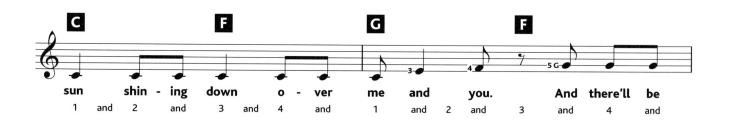

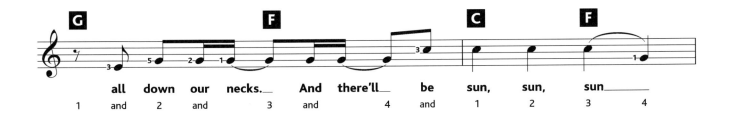

Big Yellow Taxi

Words & Music by Joni Mitchell

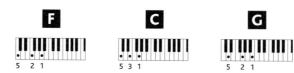

Voice: **Acoustic Guitar**
Rhythm: **Funk Rock**
Tempo: ♩ = 135

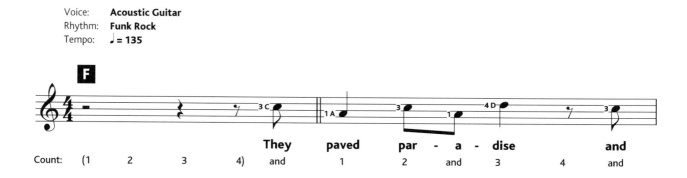

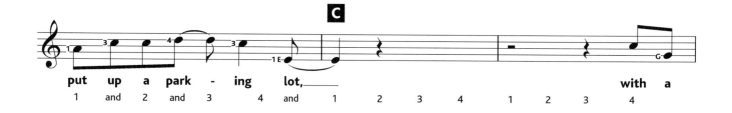

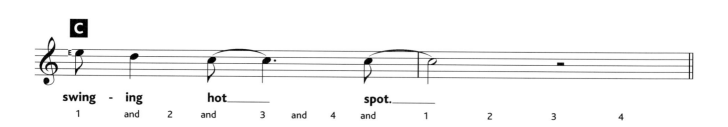

Don't it al - ways seem___ to go, that you

don't know what___ you've got___ till it's gone? They

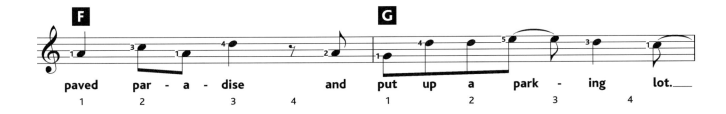

F paved par - a - dise and **G** put up a park - ing lot.___

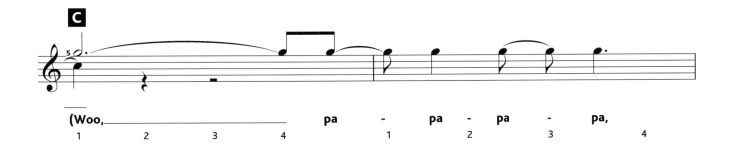

C (Woo,___ pa - pa - pa - pa,

woo,___ pa - pa - pa.)___

Chasing Cars

Words & Music by Paul Wilson, Gary Lightbody, Jonathan Quinn, Nathan Connolly & Tom Simpson

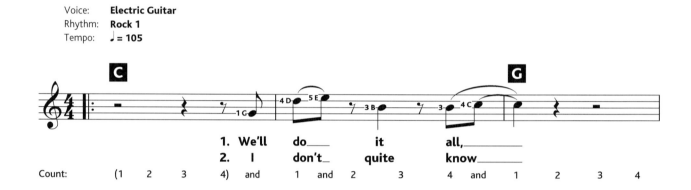

Voice: **Electric Guitar**
Rhythm: **Rock 1**
Tempo: ♩ = 105

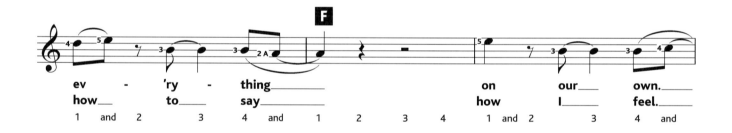

1. We'll do___ it all,_____
2. I don't__ quite know_____

Count: (1 2 3 4) and 1 and 2 3 4 and 1 2 3 4

ev - 'ry - thing_____ on our___ own.___
how___ to say_____ how I___ feel.___
1 and 2 3 4 and 1 2 3 4 1 and 2 3 4 and

___ We don't___ need_____
___ Those three___ words_____ are
1 2 3 4 1 and 2 3 4 and 1 2 3 4

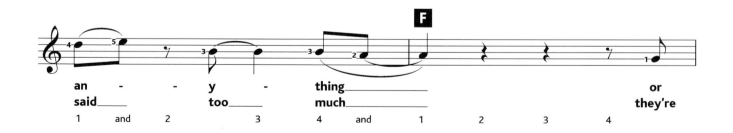

an - y - thing_____ or
said___ too___ much_____ they're
1 and 2 3 4 and 1 2 3 4

Don't Look Back In Anger

Words & Music by Noel Gallagher

Downtown

Words & Music by Tony Hatch

I Fought The Law

Words & Music by Sonny Curtis

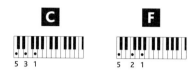

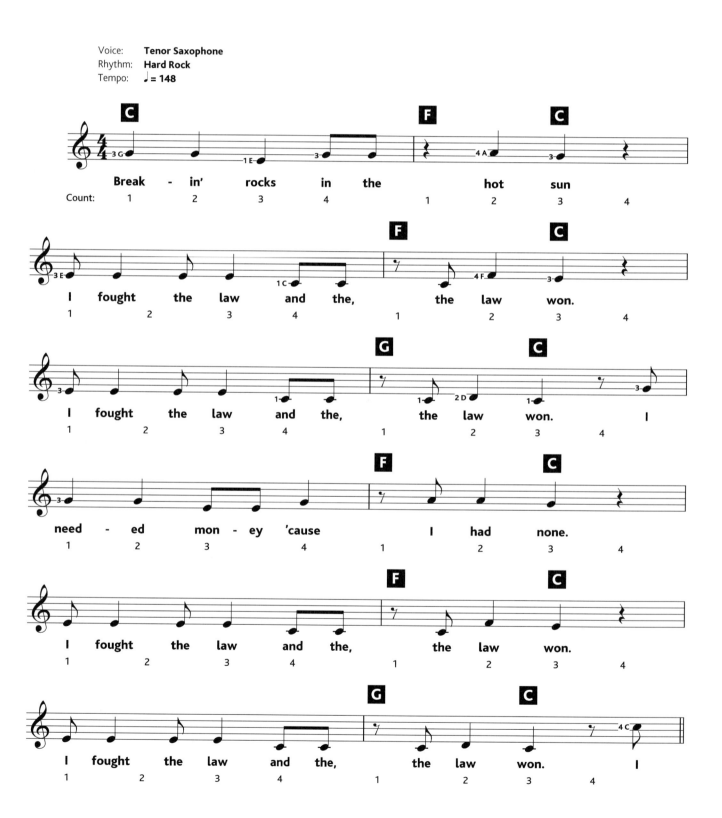

I Have A Dream

Words & Music by Benny Andersson & Björn Ulvaeus

fail.

I be - lieve in

an - gels,

some - thing good in

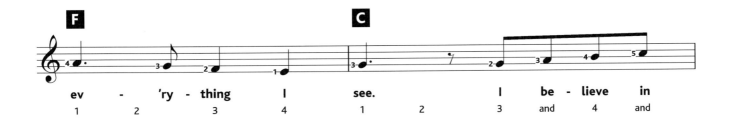

ev - 'ry - thing I see.

I be - lieve in

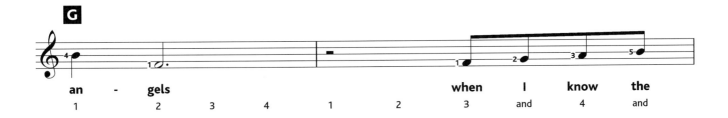

an - gels

when I know the

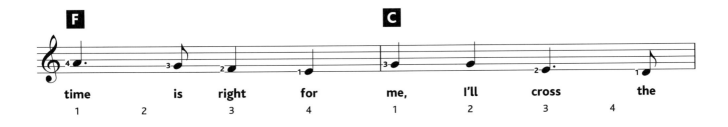

time is right for me,

I'll cross the

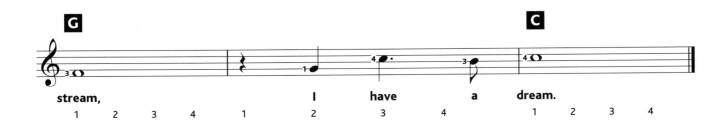

stream,

I have a dream.

I'm A Believer

Words & Music by Neil Diamond

Voice: **Electric Guitar**
Rhythm: **Beat Rock**
Tempo: ♩ = 140

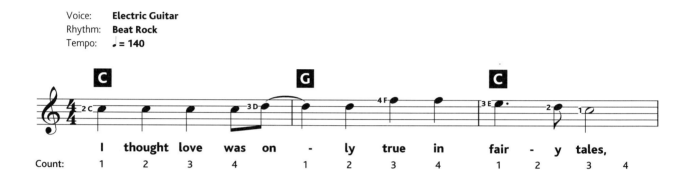

I thought love was on - ly true in fair - y tales,

Count: 1 2 3 4 1 2 3 4 1 2 3 4

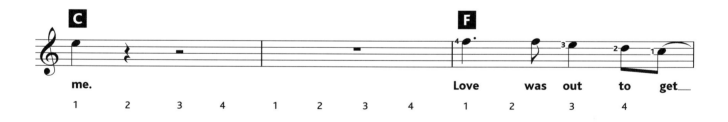

meant for some - one else___ but not___ for

1 2 3 4 1 2 3 4 1 2 3 4

me. Love was out to get___

1 2 3 4 1 2 3 4 1 2 3 4

___ me.___ That's the way it seemed.___

1 2 3 4 1 2 3 4 1 2 3 4

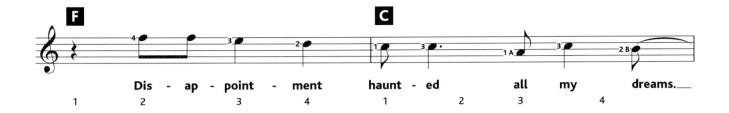

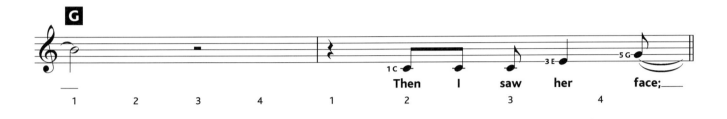

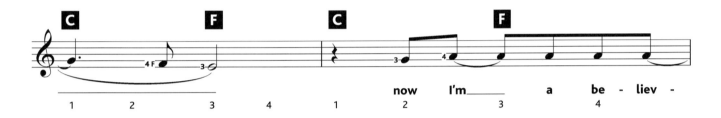

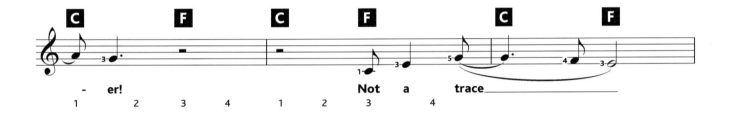

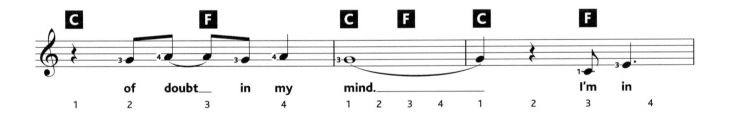

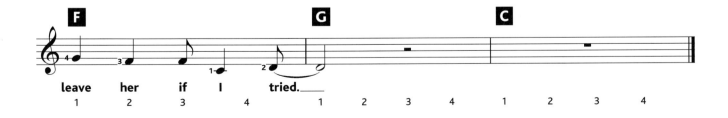

17

Knockin' On Heaven's Door

Words & Music by Bob Dylan

La Bamba

Traditional
Arranged by Ritchie Valens

Voice: **Electric Guitar**
Rhythm: **Beat Rock**
Tempo: ♩ = 120

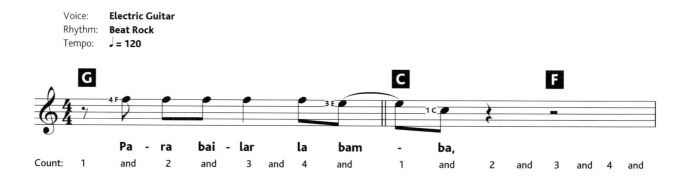

Pa – ra bai – lar la bam – ba,

Count: 1 and 2 and 3 and 4 and 1 and 2 and 3 and 4 and

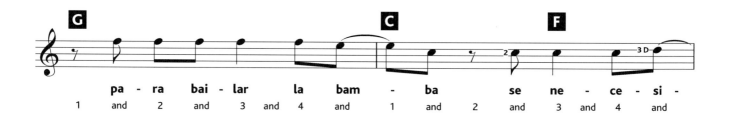

pa – ra bai – lar la bam – ba se ne – ce – si –

1 and 2 and 3 and 4 and 1 and 2 and 3 and 4 and

– ta u – na po – ca de gra – cia.

1 and 2 and 3 and 4 and 1 and 2 and 3 and 4 and

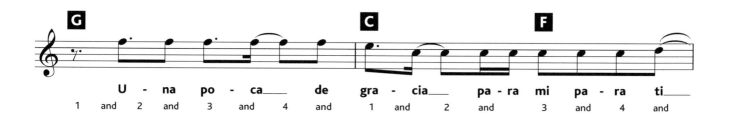

U – na po – ca___ de gra – cia___ pa – ra mi pa – ra ti___

1 and 2 and 3 and 4 and 1 and 2 and 3 and 4 and

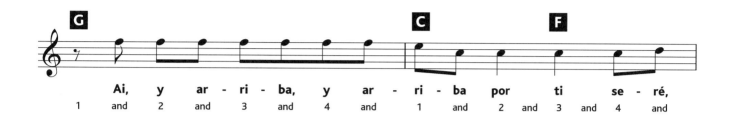

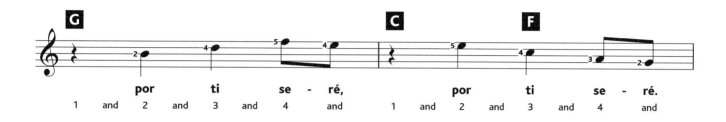

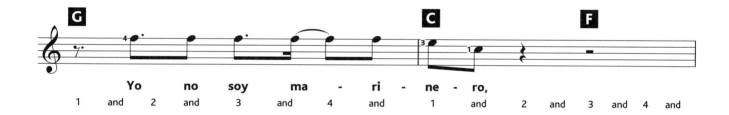

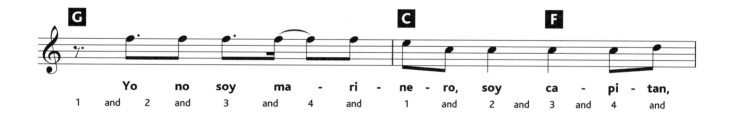

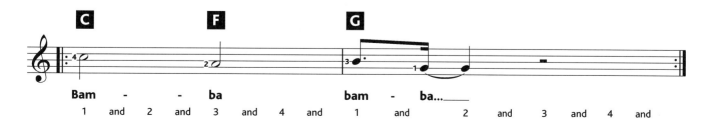

Lean On Me

Words & Music by Bill Withers

My Grandfather's Clock

Words & Music by Henry Clay Work

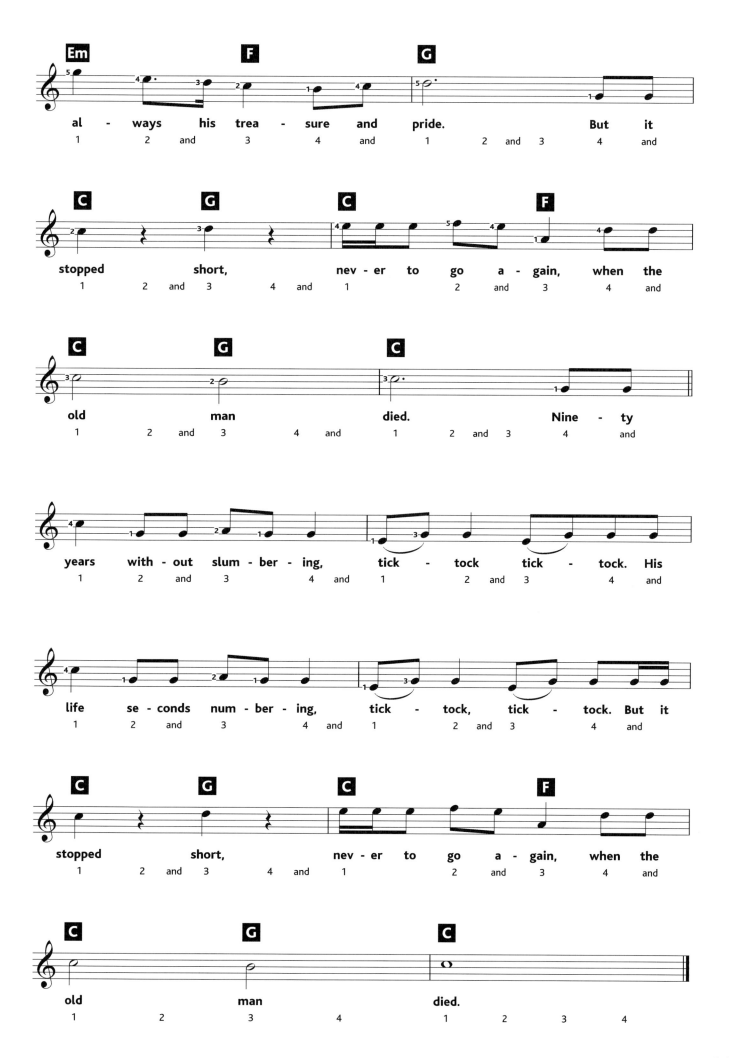

Rivers Of Babylon

Words & Music by Frank Farian, George Reyam, Brent Dowe & James McNaughton

Voice: **Marimba**
Rhythm: **Bossa Nova**
Tempo: ♩ = **110**

By the riv - ers of Bab - y - lon,_____

Count: (1) 2 and 3 and 4 and 1 2 and 3 and 4 and

where we sat down. Yeah,_____ we

1 2 and 3 and 4 and 1 2 and 3 and 4 and 1 2 and 3 and 4 and

wept, when we rem - em - bered

1 2 and 3 and 4 and 1 2 and 3 and 4 and

Zi - - on._____ By the riv - ers of

1 2 and 3 and 4 and 1 2 and 3 and 4 and

Bab - y - lon,_____ where we sat down.

1 2 and 3 and 4 and 1 2 and 3 and 4 and 1 2 and 3 and 4 and

Rolling In The Deep

Words & Music by Paul Epworth & Adele Adkins

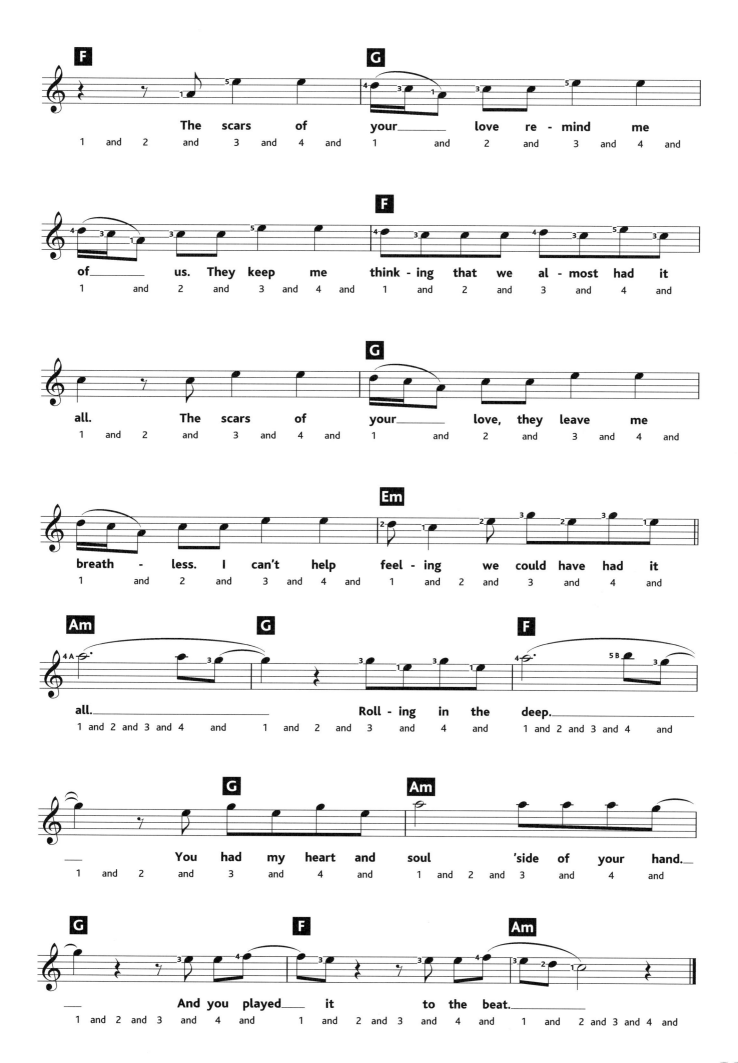

Sad Songs (Say So Much)

Words & Music by Elton John & Bernie Taupin

Voice: **Piano**
Rhythm: **Disco Pop**
Tempo: ♩ = 120

Sweet Caroline

Words & Music by Neil Diamond

Voice: **Trumpet**
Rhythm: **Shuffle Rock**
Tempo: ♩ = 150

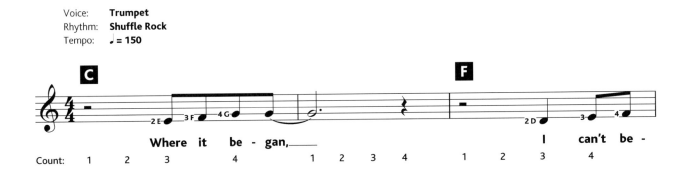

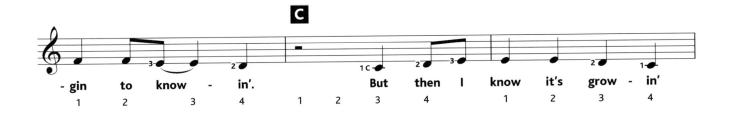

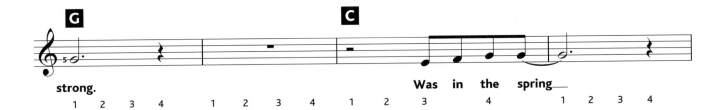

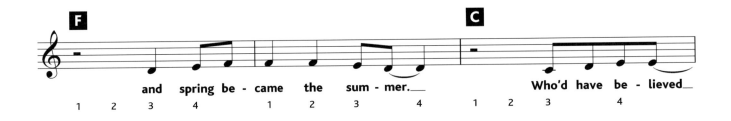

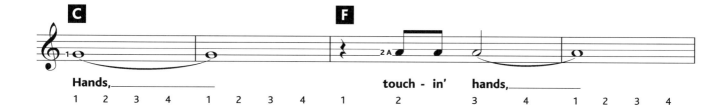

Hands, touch - in' hands,

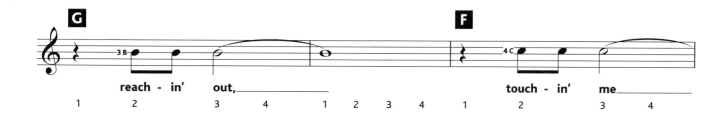

reach - in' out, touch - in' me

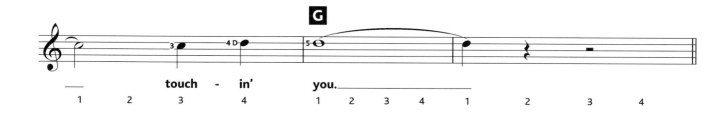

touch - in' you.

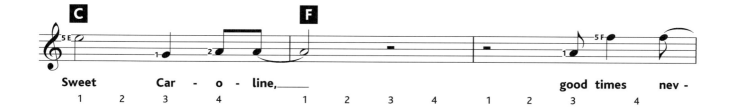

Sweet Car - o - line, good times nev -

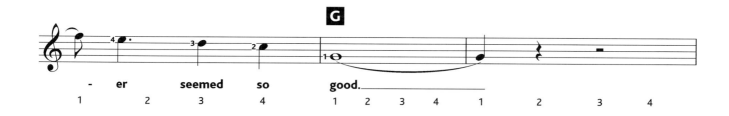

- er seemed so good.

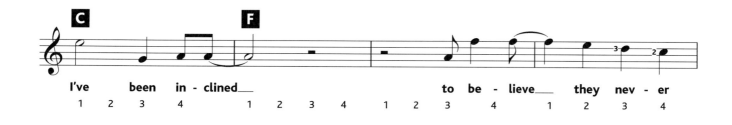

I've been in - clined to be - lieve they nev - er

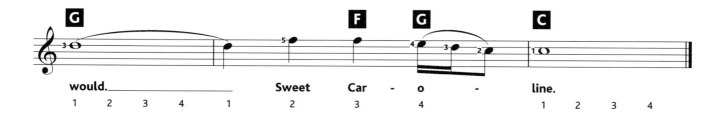

would. Sweet Car - o - line.

Twist And Shout

Words & Music by Bert Russell & Phil Medley

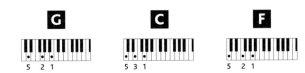

Voice: **Alto Saxophone**
Rhythm: **Beat Rock**
Tempo: ♩ = 126

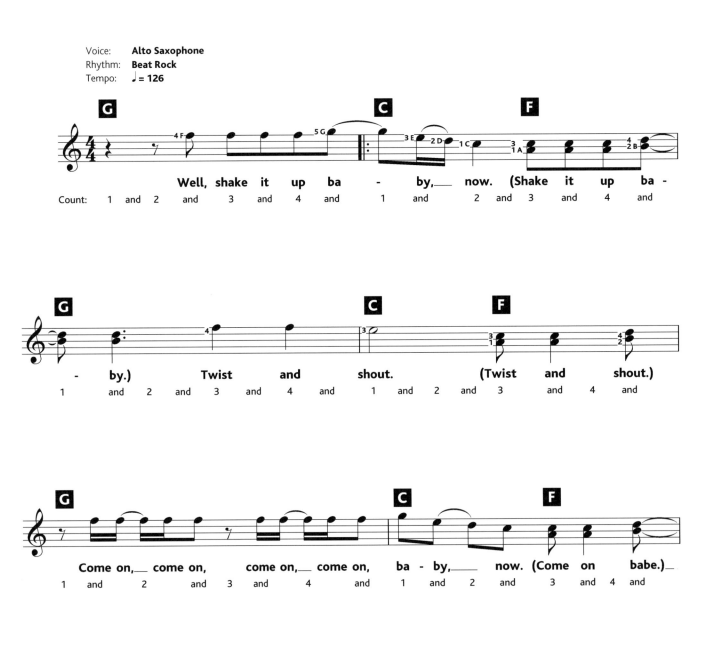

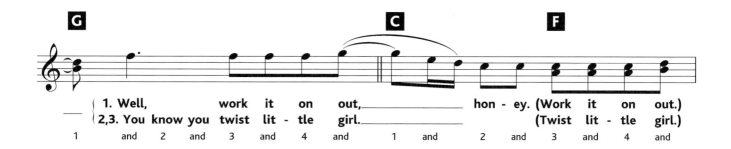

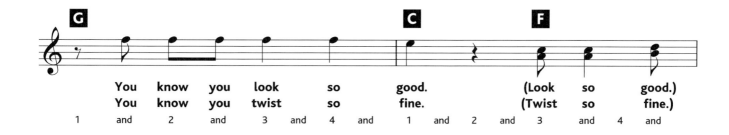

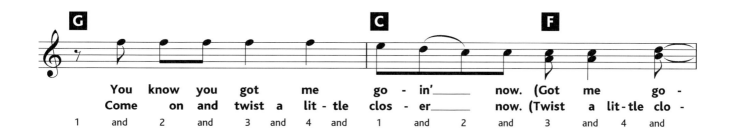

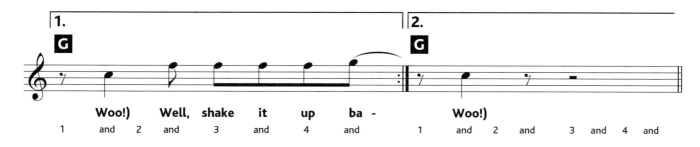

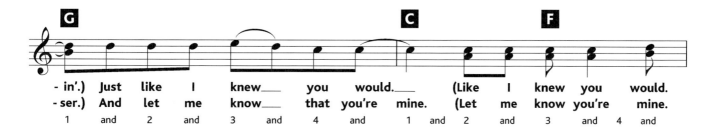

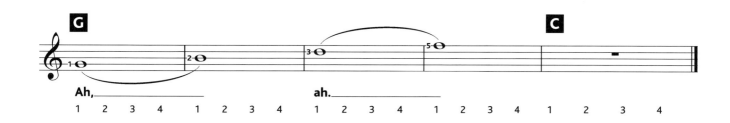

The Wild Rover

Traditional

Yellow

Words & Music by Guy Berryman, Chris Martin, Jon Buckland & Will Champion